SPIRITUAL AIDS
FOR THOSE IN RENEW

SPIRITUAL AIDS
FOR THOSE IN RENEW

Ponderings, Poems and Promises

by

**Most Reverend
Robert F. Morneau**
Auxiliary Bishop of Green Bay

ALBA · HOUSE   NEW · YORK

SOCIETY OF ST. PAUL, 2187 VICTORY BLVD., STATEN ISLAND, NEW YORK 10314

Library of Congress Cataloging in Publication Data

Morneau, Robert F., 1938-
  Spiritual aids for those in RENEW.

  1. Spiritual life—Catholic authors. I. Title.
BX2350.2.M685   1984   248.4'82   84-12299
ISBN 0-8189-0473-9

"Beginning of Friendship" by Edward Seifert, first published in
Crosscurrents.

"Grace" by Edward Seifert copyright 1984 by the Christian Century
Foundation. Reprinted by permission from the April 25, 1984 issue of
The Christian Century.

Designed, printed and bound in the United States of
America by the Fathers and Brothers of the
Society of St. Paul, 2187 Victory Boulevard,
Staten Island, New York 10314, as part of their
communications apostolate.

---

2 3 4 5 6 7 8 9 (Current Printing: first digit).

TABLE OF CONTENTS

PREFACE

The Second Vatican Council has called the Church to a process of on-going renewal. We have witnessed a deep interest in scriptural studies, the updating of the celebration of the sacraments, rich ecumenical exchange, a revitalization of prayer life, the nuanced call that the Church be in the modern world. Much has been accomplished; much remains to be done.

Several years ago the Archdiocese of Newark developed and implemented a systematic program for renewal within the Church. The program is entitled RENEW and attempts to deepen our relationship with Jesus the Lord, foster faith community and challenges us to make our faith do justice. The two and a half year program has five seasons (six weeks in each season) that stress the following themes: God's call, our response, empowerment of the Holy Spirit, discipleship and evangelization. Many dioceses around the country have taken RENEW and used it in the local church as an instrument of growth.

Our diocese here in Green Bay has benefited from the program. I personally have found it to be enriching. It also provided me with an opportunity to do some reflecting and writing on the various themes. These are accumulated in this present volume. This volume is published with the generous permission of RENEW and Paulist Press.

Also included are some poems by two friends: Ms. Barbara J. Holt and Brother Edward Seifert, F.S.C. Gratitude is due to them. Also I wish to thank Sr. Mary de Sales Hoffmann, O.S.F., Sr. Marie Isabel McElrone, O.S.F. for editorial assistance; RoseMary Bromberg for typing assistance. One last thank you: to the dedicated people on the RENEW staff.

GOD'S CALL

One Valentine Day

One Valentine's Day I received from a friend a heartshaped piece of candy on which was etched: "I love you!" Something happened to my nine-year-old heart; it jumped, it stirred, it exploded—or did something I know not what. I was different, not because of the candy, but because of the love expressed in this small, tasty gift.

God has gifted us with his love. He gives us not just life and blue skies, not just our planet earth and summer lakes, not just family and friends—he gives us himself. He calls us to open our eyes to see his nearness, to open our hearts to hear his voice in every sound, to recognize the needs of our sisters and brothers. This love has become most evident in Jesus who tells us: "As the Father has loved me, so I have loved you." (Jn 15:9)

Why are we here on earth? One poet, William Blake, sees it this way:

"And we are put on earth a little space,
That we may learn to bear the beams of love."

Our deepest need is to be loved. We are called to accept this gift and then share it with others. And God loves us as we are—warts and all! What dignity and value and worth we have. We can sing with the psalmist:

"I look up at your heavens, made by your fingers,
at the moon and stars you set in place—
ah, what is man that you should spare a thought for him,
the son of man that you should care for him?

Yet you have made him little less than a god,
you have crowned him with glory and splendor."

(Ps 8:3-5)

Don't wait for Valentine's Day either to receive love or give it as a gift. Each day God offers us his love and calls us to embrace it. When we image our God, we do the same: offer love to others and ask them to embrace it.

CHRISTMAS GIFTING

As creature of God,
  I am piece of Him,
    bit of heaven
      with earthly dirt
  and rough edges
    still remaining,
  hiding beauty beneath
    sometimes only He can see.

Yet,
  at this holy holiday time,
    I hope that gift you now hold
  is not so much me
    but presence of Christ Child within
      that you receive.
  I came into this world
    with nothing but love.
By myself I have
  no more than that
    to give you.

Barbara J. Holt

Humpty Dumpty's Dilemma

The Lord calls us in our individual difficulties and says he will heal.

Old Humpty Dumpty sat too high on the wall and broke apart when he fell off and hit the ground. And the large question: who would put Humpty Dumpty back together again?

Life has many difficulties—high walls which sometimes cause falls in our lives: strained relationships between parents and children; doubts about one's own worth; confusion about what one should do in life; failures in friendships; sin that alienates and causes guilt and pain. Life is tough and when things are not going well our faith tends to weaken and God seems so distant. Whatever the case, there is suffering. As one proverb reminds us: "Whether the knife falls on the melon or the melon on the knife, the melon suffers."

What is God's attitude toward the melon, whether its suffering is self-inflicted or caused from the outside? God desires our healing and wholeness. He longs to reconcile all of creation to himself. So Jesus came to bring healing and peace, mercy and forgiveness, consolation and strength. If all the king's horses and men could not put Humpty Dumpty back together again, Jesus can.

Jesus knows the difficulties of life from the inside: he was physically beaten and killed; he was betrayed and rejected; he sensed abandonment and temptation. In all of this, he was obedient in accepting and doing the Father's will. Just as he healed the leper and the blind man, just as he forgave the adulterous woman and the self-righteous Pharisees, just as he bore the grief of Peter's denial and Judas' betrayal, so he comes to us in our sickness, sin and failure. And he comes with a love that we call mercy.

Life is difficult. Our God comes to us to bear our burden. In this is our salvation and joy.

PAIN

You will never be as alone as now
In the sudden flare and stab of it
There in your side where the ribs sit.
You live in the strictest privacy
You will ever be knowing.
No hand can soothe, no mind can reach
The darkened cage where you toss.
The stabs are staggered. You never know
The exact time of the knife.
You have learned too well that your pain
Is yours, inalienably yours.
This evil you have learned to claim
As yours, undeniably yours,
Even as a harassed father must claim
His basest child and most hideous.

Edward Seifert, F.S.C.

The Domestic Church

"There's no place like home!" So reads the familiar banner. It is in the home, the domestic church, that family life is nurtured and sustained. When love is present, all the members of the family have the chance of growing—when there is indifference and fear, family life is stunted and sometimes destroyed.

A family is a community, a group of people called together by God to care for one another, to share common values, to be committed to a life style that respects everyone. A Christian family or community is aware that Christ is present to strengthen and encourage that family to be loving and forgiving and caring.

Three symbols tell of the quality of Christian life. One is the TABLE. What happens at table will set the tone of family life. If there is good communication and more than just a sharing of food at table, growth takes place. In that communication which involves prayer, a sharing of ideas, a respect for each other, a community of parents, children and friends are enriched.

A second symbol is the DOORMAT. Some doormats have the word "Welcome" on them which indicates to visitors that when they enter through the door they will receive gracious hospitality. The mat is worn well in allowing friends and strangers to find peace and refuge.

But just as important is to note how worn the mat is in the outgoing direction. Do members of the family leave the home to assist others who are in need: the sick in the hospital, the poor who need clothing and food, the bereaved who hunger for consolation? Hospitality and service characterize a Christian household.

A third symbol: the CRUCIFIX. Christian families are more than just a human community, more than just a service community—they are also a faith community. The cross symbolizes the redeeming love of God that sustains and surrounds us. Jesus is the wisdom and power helping us to see and do the loving thing.

Community building is not easy. Family life demands grace; the grace of commitment.

LEARNING

From you I have learned awareness:
In the lift of a man's arm kindness,
In the blind a deeper vision,
In the voice on the telephone breath
And pulse of friendship.

From you I have learned that a feast
Can enrich a month of fasting,
How script on a looseleaf page
Can be treasured like pearls on velvet.

And from me you have learned not patience
But the quiet heart's forebearance,
How to make of age a transmuter
Of time into gold.

Edward Seifert, F.S.C.

Lest The Parish Perish

Christian families cluster together in a given territory and form a parish. Under the guidance of a pastor, the people of God are called upon to worship, to teach and to serve. Jesus is present in this community constantly calling us to live in love, peace and harmony.

A parish prays together. With awe and reverence, we gather for Eucharist and the other sacraments in deep faith. God is praised for the mystery that he is, thanked for all the gifts that he bestows. A true parish takes nothing for granted knowing full well that all is grace. Public and personal prayer connect us with the source of life and continually deepen our relationship with the Father, Son and Spirit.

A parish teaches. Without the mysteries cf faith and solid knowledge of doctrine we become disoriented and the meaning of life is obscured. We need vision; the truths articulated by the Church provide guidance and direction. Such teaching not only nourishes our minds; it also expands our hearts and calls us to action. Relationships can only grow if built on truth. Thus we invest much time and energy and money in our educational ministry. This ministry moves beyond our faith community by means of evangelization.

A parish serves. Jesus came not to be served but to serve. As his people we are not afraid to recognize and develop our gifts in meeting the needs of our brothers and sisters. Baptism calls all of us into ministry and to stewardship. God has entrusted much to us and much will be expected. Our discipleship in the Lord is characterized by service.

When a parish functions as a family there will be cooperation and affection, deep sharing and dialogue. There will also be tensions and conflicts. In all this we are to remember that the Lord is with us. With the eyes of faith we can recognize his presence and respond to his call.

A THOUSAND FACES

What does it mean to us
Kneeling like this before the One
Of a thousand faces,
Not a thousand but unnumbered thousands?
His color is my color,
His accent is my accent
Here as on this cliff edge he holds me
Overlooking creation's chasm.
His tone is your tone also, your likeness
His likeness there as he holds you
Up close as though you were the one man living.

His children he has fathered
And loved each of them riding
The waves of onrolling time.
Each star of his galaxies he has pressed
Close to his bosom,
Each star, each child he has loved
As though it were the one star glittering.

Edward Seifert, F.S.C.

He Ain't Heavy . . .

"He ain't heavy, Father, he's my brother!" That well-known seal and expression contains a paradox: physically the younger brother being carried is heavy but because of love, the burden is lightened so as to almost be forgotten.

The Lord calls us to love—to love him and our neighbor as ourself. The summons is always supported by the offer of grace. God is the one who helps us create peaceful, life-giving relationships. The task is not easy because of certain pitfalls. Three of them are mistrust, isolation and anger.

A poster showing a camera peering down at a customer making a deposit at a bank window reads: "In God we trust, everyone else we watch very carefully." Indeed we are to trust God but also we are to trust one another though this necessarily involves the risk of getting hurt. We trust when we allow others to make decisions, accept responsibility, use their gifts. Without such trust, love cannot exist. It turns into a subtle form of manipulation and control.

Loneliness is often caused by isolation. Some people continually ask: "Who really cares?" Mr. Scrooge in Dickens' *Christmas Carol* was isolated because he did not love. Once he dared to reach out a whole new life awaited him. Reaching out to the poor, lonely, abandoned is central to the gospel message. The joy that results cannot be measured either by the giver or the recipient.

The Lord's call to love one's neighbor faces a third pitfall: anger. Cain was angry that Abel's offering was accepted; that anger led to murder. The elder brother of the prodigal son was angry at the warm, merciful welcome by the father; that anger engendered alienation. Such anger is in need of the grace of humility, reverence and joy to remove its sting and poison.

One function we have as Church is to make Jesus' love

present to our sisters and brothers. What a vocation! What a responsibility!

PITFALLS

Body wanders about,
  dabbling in this or that—
  water plants—
    straighten sofa pillows—
  put away clothes—
  take out bus tickets for tomorrow
any thing
  to prevent mind
    from quieting down
      long enough
  to decide what to do
      next,
    which road to take,
      whose path to follow.
Many opportunities
  hold forth eager hands
  overflowing with dreamy ideas
  which can,
      like sand,
  slip through fingers.
To hold it once—
    and free it?
Or to hold too tight—
    and lose it?

Barbara J. Holt

Characterless Caterpillar

A caterpillar was journeying through the tall summer grass when he and his companion spotted a butterfly circling high in the August winds. After a slight pause the caterpillar said to his buddy: "You could not get me up into one of those things for a million dollars!"

Our poor caterpillar lacked two graces that are essential to a full life: hope and courage. Hope allows us to see the possibilities of things even though they might seem to be highly unlikely. Courage is that virtue that empowers us to face trials and difficulties with strength.

Hope is grounded in God and in his promise to be with us always. He never promised his disciples a rose garden or cheap grace. The cost of discipleship is high. Our hope is nourished by an enduring love offering a peace and joy that no one can take away. Even when sin and death touch our journey, we turn to Jesus who gives us hope through his cross and resurrection. Indeed hope overcomes all fears.

Courage may well be called "the lost virtue" in our century. Fortitude demands that we plant our feet when suffering comes our way. Flight and fright are well practiced in our day; courage and perseverance are endangered species.

Two sources of courage for us are found in the word of God and the sacraments. Here we encounter in special ways the risen Lord who is our strength. His word encourages our faltering hearts and his sacraments empower our drooping spirits. So strengthened, we grow in our ability to lay down our lives for one another.

Recovered hope is always grounded in love. God's extravagant love is always available. God is love; he cannot not love. To stand in the warmth of his Son instills new life and hope—how graced and blessed we are.

HOPE AND COURAGE

Today
held such pleasures
    beyond expectations,
of which there were
        none,
but,
    even so,
        such delights
amidst meetings,
    both planned and sudden,
at work, in home,
    from people—
wonders above creation
    since each
        becomes their own
            person/creator,
with each new dawn
    being fresh beginning
in clean sketch book
    using unpeeled crayons
or uncapped oils.
    Create,
        artist friends!

                                        Barbara J. Holt

OUR RESPONSE

Look Before You Leap

In July, 1941, Father Maximilian Kolbe took a risk. He was prisoner 16,670 in Auschwitz. During a reprisal Maximilian Kolbe stepped forth and offered to take the place of a selected victim, Franciszek Gajownicek who was a husband and father. Father Kolbe died a few weeks later, injected with carbolic acid after two weeks of starvation. He risked his life! On October 10, 1982, Maximilian Kolbe was canonized.

Life is risky: the risk a child takes in getting on a bicycle for the first time; the risk of visiting a prison or a dying person and not knowing what to say; the risk of extending an invitation of friendship with the possibility of rejection; the risk of being baptized into the life of Jesus Christ. Such reaching out involves the possibility of failure. It also presents a glorious opportunity for a fuller life. Self-protection behind neatly constructed defense mechanisms; self-commitment that may well cost us our lives? We must choose!

Jesus took many 'chances' in his life. He invited fishermen to become his disciples and continue his mission; he challenged the leaders and elders regarding their interpretation of the scriptures; he visited the homes of sinners and befriended those who were outcasts from society. We know what happened because of these 'risky' choices. Oftentimes he was rejected and abandoned; oftentimes he became the object of hatred; oftentimes he was ridiculed and scorned. Yet he did not withdraw from his work of bringing the Father's love and forgiveness to all. The mission of the kingdom elicited total commitment and fidelity, whatever the risk.

A Catholic novelist and short-story writer, Flannery O'Connor, once wrote: "All human nature vigorously resists grace because grace changes us and the change is painful." As we look into our own lives and realize the moments of God's gracious intrusions we may well discover many times of resistance. The security of comforts, a long standing attitude, a treasured position, an exclusive friendship may have become subtle idols. We resist the invitation to let go. Yet when grace won out and we took the chance of doing God's will and not our own, new life poured into our hearts.

RENEW is a risky process. It demands a change of mind and heart; it involves us in matters of justice and peace; it challenges us to a deeper knowledge and love of the Lord. As the preface of our Eucharistic celebration prays: "We do well always and everywhere to give you thanks." St. Maximilian Kolbe offered this prayer many, many times. Let us too thank the Lord for the risks which he sends into our lives. They are indeed an invitation and an adventure in grace.

BEGINNING OF FRIENDSHIP

Beginning is always the best:
The instant knowing,
The twist of the dial to gladness,
The stepping out to a clearing flanked by trees
Eerily new but familiar.
You have been there before. You remember the light
As you see the smile that steals into you.
You take his hand remembering the hands
Stretched out to you in old mornings.
This is best, you say, as out of memory
You step out with him into the daylight.

Brother Edward Seifert, F.S.C.

Moral Cancer

The word "cancer" causes our hearts and bodies to shudder. Life is threatened and we immediately seek the help of the medical professional to arrest this harbinger of death. In some cases the cancer is more superficial and can be dealt with without great damage to our health; in other cases, it is terminal and snuffs out life.

In our moral and spiritual life there are also certain "cells" that cause destruction, division and death. These cells are sin: free choices made in opposition to God's plan of love, justice and peace. Sin severs! It ruptures our relationship with God, with one another and even with ourself. We become alienated and isolated, blind and deaf to the great mysteries of life. Like cancer there are various degrees and kinds of sin but all of them threaten the life of Christ given to us in baptism.

One thing is certain: we cannot afford to ignore sin. If we do everything is in jeopardy. The challenge here is to honesty and humility. With grace we must live in the truth of things and turn to God for healing. An acronym, NCT, may be helpful in meeting that challenge.

N = naming! The first thing to be done with sin is to name it. PRIDE: attributing to ourselves gifts that come from God. ENVY: that feeling of discontent and ill will because of the advantages or possessions that others have. GREED: excessive desire for acquiring and having more than one needs. IN-JUSTICE: depriving others of their rights or not fulfilling one's duties. On first glance this may seem easy but in daily life it can be most difficult. It takes courage to call by name that fundamental posture of turning away from God and to label those specific deeds which are not of God's Spirit. This threatens our ego and self-respect.

C = claiming! Naming is not enough. We must also claim our sin as indeed our own. This means taking responsibility for those deeds which separate us from God and others. It also means taking ownership for those omissions which happen when we refuse to respond to what God is asking us in his commandments and the teaching of the Church. We cannot afford to take out that too common T-shirt which is inscribed: "The Devil Made Me Do It!" Rather, we etch on our T-shirt: "I Take Full Responsibility for What I Have Done or Not Done!"

T = taming! A third step in the process of dealing with sin is to TAME it. This however is not primarily our work. After naming our sin and assuming responsibility for it, we go to the Lord for his mercy and forgiveness. Grace tames, heals, restores. Grace brings about conversion and repentance. Without grace we are powerless in the face of sin. Indeed, the very naming and claiming is itself the work of the Spirit in our lives. Throughout the journey God is with us, his people. Not only in those times in which we live in light but he comes to us in the darkness of our individual and collective sin with his healing touch.

Malignant cancer means death. Here the analogy ends: malignant sin need not mean death if we turn to the Lord and ask pardon. No game playing here. We go to the divine physician through the sacrament of reconciliation and receive absolution. Such a journey is at the heart of our RENEW program.

THE SHADOW

I

They who have loved me have seen my shadow,
The fearsome length of it,
Tailing me as I go about my blithe business.
They have seen it dog me on all these brave mornings
When I did not see the sprawl of it
Like a bush moving.

It is with me but I have not seen it mirrored
In this glass where I stand,
And they who have loved me feared to disturb
Me with the news of integral evil
And let it move in as I prayed and praised God
And greeted my guests at the doorstep.
A spectre? No, not a spectre,
But around and within me,
Indivisibly I.

II

But one who has loved me, the youngest and kindest,
Drew near half in anger and said:
"I love you yet cannot love you
Because of the thing that shadows and warps you,
Making you half-unlovely.
We have learned, for your shadow has told us,
That it is not we you have loved
But the pleasure we bore you
And the comfort we laid on you there
As you circled us with your greetings."

You, the youngest and kindest,
     have stamped on my shadow and cursed it,
Not knowing that by naming the Evil
You blessed me
And in your firm way have empowered me
To face without fear that dark Presence.

Brother Edward Seifert, F.S.C.

Raised Eyebrows

Most of life is conditional: health is dependent upon proper nourishment, rest and exercise. A person gets paid for a job *if* the work is accomplished. The student will do well in an examination in proportion to the amount of study and preparation. Life is filled with If . . . Then! Thus when we hear the expression that something is unconditional (no ifs, ands or buts . . .) our eyebrows are raised in disbelief.

Yet, in recent years, we have all heard the expression that God has unconditional love for us. Another way of saying this is that God cannot not love and still be God. St. John writes in his epistle that "God is love." What a mystery—to have a God of extravagant and unconditional love.

What about our raised eyebrows? There seems to be in the expression of unconditional love an inner paradox. St. Luke's gospel which tells the story of the prodigal son may be of some help. In the story the abandoned father has a love for his wayward son that is unconditional. The love is in his heart and nothing can remove it, not even the life style of his son. Prodigality does not destroy this paternal love. Yet something happened when the son left the father's house and land—he walked away from that love and chose to live in the darkness and coldness of his sin. The son walked away from the embrace of the father; the father would not force that loving embrace on his son. Although the father's love was unconditional, there was a *condition* that the son had to deal with—he needed to turn around (repentance) and walk back to his father's embrace. The unconditional love of the father was constant; its reception was conditioned upon the son's disposition and choice.

Would that our human loves were as gracious and as unconditional as that of God our Father. We interject so many qualifications on our loves: *if* you are good to me *then* I will love you; *if* you are grateful for what I have done for you *then* I will continue our friendship; *if* you come and ask for forgiveness *then* I might consider pardoning you. Such game playing is not of the Spirit. God's love is constant and faithful, always available to anyone who turns to him with open heart.

As kids in grade school we, in the spring of the year, would play the "daisy game." Finding a fresh daisy we would pull out the petals one by one with the ardent concern: "She loves me! She loves me not!" The great hope would be that the last petal would contain the refrain: "She loves me!" How else for grade school kids to discern the heart of a friendship.

At times we play this daisy game with God: "He loves me! He loves me not!" Such a fickle God—a God who is in and out of love dependent on the behavior of humankind—is not the God that Jesus reveals to us. The Father of Jesus has a love that is overwhelming, extravagant and faithful. Yes, Unconditional!

UNCONDITIONAL LOVE

He'll love me enough
to let me be free
  yet strong enough
   to let me need him
and love him,
  letting him go
while letting him know
   home is always waiting
    in my arms
     and in my soul.
He'll care as much
   for others
as he cares for me,
   giving them his time
when he'd rather
  be with me—
  and tells me so.
He'll say "no"
  when he has to,
   when he doesn't want to,
   when he knows it'll make me grow—
Help me love you the same—

Barbara J. Holt

Fill In The Blank

In seventh grade I began thinking about what I wanted to do with my life. Being in a quandary, I sought the Lord's help. Before going to bed one evening I took out a piece of paper and neatly listed several options:

_____ 1. Farmer (like the dad of one of my classmates)
_____ 2. Doctor (like my own father)
_____ 3. Green Bay Packer (like Tobin Rote)
_____ 4. whatever you want, God (fill-in).

On my bedstand I set the paper with a sharpened pencil and in my night prayer said: "O.K., God, mark the one you want or fill in the last blank." Next morning the paper and pencil still rested in silence.

Such are the discerning ways of a thirteen year old boy. Decisions of life are somewhat more complex than the above process. God has given us the great gift of freedom which allows *us* to select the road of life that we will travel. The options for the Christian are many as to specific vocations; yet there is one basic vocation that flows from our baptism: to follow the mind and heart of Christ Jesus. We call that decision one of discipleship.

Life is tough, so too our decisions. Part of the difficulty is that every serious decision contains a commitment. The Christian decision of discipleship gives us a "master concern" (commitment) around which all other interests and values are subordinated. In an attempt to hang on to many interests and values and relationships, some people never make a radical commitment and face a life of dissipation and often disorientation. Those who make a commitment to and for the Lord come into singleness of heart, a gospel value of no small price.

God has made a commitment to us: he is our God and we

are his people. Here, in this gift of covenant and fidelity, we find our model. Our challenge is to commit ourselves to his work and ways. We are to build up the kingdom by being instruments of life and truth, holiness and grace, love and justice and peace. Such a road is narrow and steep; such a road is filled with joy and happiness.

In the sport of kayaking, decisions must be constantly made as one travels through the rapids and around the boulders in the river. Two terms express poor choices on the river run: 1) *static clunk*: a person who while kayaking does nothing in a critical situation; 2) *dynamic clunk*: a person who while kayaking does the wrong thing in a critical situation. Kayaking is not unlike Christianity in that it is a journey that demands constant decisions. The crises in life are many and we cannot avoid not to do anything nor can we avoid to do the wrong thing. With God's grace and deep personal commitment our decision will be based on discerning God's word in our everyday situation and responding in courage and generosity.

Shakespeare once suggested that the basic question in life is to be or not to be! Important as that question is a more pragmatic question in everyday life is to do or not to do . . . the will of God!

DECISION

Between the spring bird and Church
I sat—one ear on the Robin's song,
One on more solemn human notes.
Torn between, my heart faltered.

How many sat thus?
Dickinson surely, Joyce—all Emersons,
These ran from the window, altar forgone,
Others sang in choirs: Augustine—Paul.

Can the inbetween be held?
Traitor to both but true to oneself?
A lonely perch—a different song,
A love of all—loyal to life.

Robert F. Morneau

Where Do You Live?

The first line of an old Latin song read: "Ubi caritas et amor, Deus ibi est!" (Where charity and love are, there God is!) Ubi=where; ibi=there. Throughout history the search for where God lives has been great. This song gives us a brilliant clue; God is present wherever authentic love dwells. A basic call in the RENEW program is to experience that presence of God and make His love available to others.

Several summers ago I asked an owl where he lived and he quickly responded that his home was in Sullivan's woods. I asked him a second time: "Where do you really live?" That "wise" owl was unable to tell me that he lived in the air. The same thing happened to a large Coho salmon that I extracted from Lake Michigan this past August. Upon being asked where he lived (his response: "I used to live in Lake Michigan!") he was unable to tell me that his home was water. The bird is so surrounded by air, the fish by water, that they lack consciousness of their environment. We too answer like our fellow creatures: "I live in Taos or Beaver Dam or Antigo!" Do we realize that we live in God, surrounded and sustained by his loving presence?

Such awareness is difficult because of the daily concerns and activities of our lives. Though our faith continually reminds us that God's redeeming love is ever present the reality of this mystery strikes home only on occasion: the occasion of an unusual event. RENEW as a process tries to help focus on the mystery of God's abiding presence.

Certain spiritual exercises help to recall that God is near: moments of quiet reflection, prayers at the start of events (the day, a meal, a meeting) and at their closing, the affirmation of a friend, the surprise letter or phone call. God's presence can be found in all these human experiences as well as in our sacraments and scripture, our tradition and history, the subtle movements of our hearts. If our antennae are sensitive, we begin to feel his presence, hear his word, feel his touch. Upon such awareness a response is called for.

Where is God? That question continues to haunt every generation. As a community of faith, as a Church, we must help to provide an answer for those who question. By our love and concern they will find God because God is wherever there is love. The deeper our awareness of the Lord, the better chance we have of being fit instruments to share in his mission.

St. Paul would challenge us "to live through love in his presence." This presence is one of truth, charity, freedom, justice and peace. Indeed, "Ubi caritas et amor, Deus ibi est!"

GOD'S ABIDING PRESENCE

God,
   I've discovered your favorite,
the tree you like
   best of all,
for You bless its branches
   with budding filigree
      in springtime
so it can ever so slowly unfold
   its treasure of life
      toward You,
         and me,
   walking beneath Your tree.
Shade is gently spread
   during hot summer months,
      giving cool space
   between humid places,
patch of peaceful breeze
      to please passerby.
And walking into winter,
   one passes through autumn,
THE time when
   Your own
   bring forth
      in beauty and splendor
color combinations
      and intensities
   no other artist
would even dream
      or attempt
         to create—
yet it happens every day

outside windows,
 along streets
  and country roads.
Yes,
 your secret
  is over—
I *know*!

Barbara J. Holt

Learn A Lesson From The Redwood

In certain moist valleys of California, giant redwood trees tower to the sky like church steeples. Some of them are two hundred years old and have been in a process of growth and renewal for all that time. A lesson can be learned in these forests: great acts take time; renewal is an ongoing process; we must have perseverance, enthusiasm and hope.

Jesus' invitation to discipleship begins a life-long process of conversion. As God's life is given to us, we continually discover new unredeemed areas of our lives. In so doing we can become discouraged. We get tired of constantly having to change and renew ourselves. Inertia moves in to claim dominion. What is needed is the gift of *perseverance*—that power of staying with this life regardless of the weather. The redwood trees face a variety of days: sunshine and storms, heat and cold, disease and health. But always the process of life and renewal continues, or at least the call. At times the tendency to quit and throw in the towel will be activated. In these moments we face a crisis (turning point). If we persevere, that turning point can be a rich opportunity to the next level of development.

Another quality that is essential to renewal is *enthusiasm*. One author has labeled this the "master virtue." Enthusiasm brings a freshness and vibrancy to our relationships and daily lives. A certain spark animates our words; a tender glance enkindles weary hearts; a soft touch consoles the depressed. The Spirit of God permeates our being allowing us to bring life to others and to end their exiles. Such a Spirit is contagious and enriches the community. Renewal is not possible without enthusiasm.

Emily Dickinson once wrote that *hope* "is the thing with feathers, that perches in the soul." Renewal is based on a promise and an expectation. We have been promised fullness of life; we expect that God is faithful to his word. Our hope is that the kingdom that Jesus proclaimed will come. Because of this great possibility we are energized to make our contribution. As a gift, hope has been given; as a task, we must allow this bird not only to warm our own souls but to brood over the entire world. We do pray that the Spirit will renew the face of the earth.

As the redwood trees provide us with a lesson of on-going renewal so do wine and cheese, both demanding many seasons to reach their full potential. Wine cannot afford to go flat; nor cheese stale. This was the fear of two mice who were on their way to a birthday party for a friend. As they passed through the hole in the wall and entered the guest room, a large table was filled with all kinds of wine and cheese. One of the mice turned to his buddy and said: "Oh, no, not another wine and cheese party!" Indeed, the best laid schemes of mice and men can go awry. Our renewal can go flat; it can become stale unless we have hope, enthusiasm and perseverance. These graces provide the wine and bread that bring full life.

GREATER THAN WE KNEW

Even as the poet tells us,
They were greater than we knew,
These men who stood among us
Growing to the stature
Only God has measured.
Kindness was for them a natural
Outreach, free and open
As the plant that flowers.
They have lived among us
Wise and simple men,
Spreading their gifts and talents
As the maple spreads its boughs,
These men of love and valor
Who were greater than we knew.

Brother Edward Seifert, F.S.C.

EMPOWERMENT OF THE SPIRIT

You Do What?

Job descriptions! The very term can elicit mixed emotions. Yet every teacher, administrator, coach, catechist, parent has a specific role to play in an important area of life. Job descriptions attempt to articulate what the duties and responsibilities are as we live in community. At times these roles escape precise wording but it is important to attempt to clarify as much as possible what we are about so that we might understand how to live life as fully as possible. Yet who would dare draw up a job description for God and the working of the Spirit within history?

Perhaps only hints and clues are available and we turn to scripture for these. Walter Bruggemann, a well-known scripture scholar, formulates his understanding of God in the Bible as being a God who is a life-giver, an exile-ender and a freedom-bringer. The job description that the word of God provides for us spells out these functions as the unique ways in which grace (God's life) comes to us.

Life-giving! Jesus came to bring us the fullness of life: the dead are raised, the crippled are healed, the broken-hearted are consoled. Jesus is *the* life-giver. His ministry and mission have been given to us and with that call comes the gift of the Holy Spirit. The Spirit, working in us, continues the work of Jesus that the Father sent him to accomplish. The Spirit's role is to call us from all the darkness and sin that destroys life into a life-style that brings life and grace to others. Made to the image and likeness of God, we are to be life-givers and the presence of the Spirit in our lives makes that possible.

Exile-ending! Jesus came to reconcile all creation to the Father. He came to bring us home. Through his words and life the Father's mercy and forgiveness reach our fragile and broken world with healing power. The Spirit of Jesus and the Father continues to bring unity and oneness into our lives. Our exiles, caused by arrogant isolation, by needless divisions, by sinful alienation, are the object of his merciful touch. We are given that Spirit so that as Church we might extend that exile-ending activity in our local circumstances.

Freedom-bringing! The resurrection of Jesus has broken the bonds of death and sin. Powerless in the face of these two tragic realities, we gain power by identifying with our Lord in all the mysteries of his life. The freedom won through resurrection is a call to serious responsibility. The Lord wants us to live mature lives of faith that focus on proclaiming and bringing about the kingdom. It is a freedom of commitment; it is a freedom of discipleship; it is a freedom of love. Any other freedom is license.

The Spirit is given to us through the instrumentality of the Church. The "job description" for every Christian is based on the role of the Holy Spirit. Our task is the same as that of Jesus and is the same one given to the apostles on Pentecost day: "Be life-givers; be exile-enders; be freedom-bringers!" Continue in history the mysteries of Jesus' incarnation, redemption and resurrection. Hopefully we will all hear those glorious words: "Well done, good and faithful servant. Enter the kingdom of my Father." The job description has been fulfilled.

GRACE

It comes as a shining girl
On a bicycle riding straight toward you.
Without stopping she throws a smile
Meant just for you
Alone on the roadway.
She has seen you and out of her bowl of gladness
Sprinkled you that morning
As you sagged there on the roadway.
You will not see her again, the shining girl
And the wheels aiming right at you,
But you will go to your rooms and take
Your rest at midday
And the grace of the riding girl
Will grow a tall flower beside you.

Brother Edward Seifert, F.S.C.

The Power And The Glory

Flower power! Economic power! Fear power! Love power! Spirit power!

POWER: that basic ability to bring about or to prevent change. The word itself stirs up deep emotions in all of us, positive or negative, depending upon our individual experience. For some, power is a dread force intruding upon freedom and human rights; for others, power is a constructive force leading to growth and development. For still others, power is a mixed blessing.

Our faith reveals that the Spirit of God has power to bring about the transformation of the human heart and of our world. We pray that the Spirit might renew the face of the earth making it radiant with love and forgiveness. That renewal indicates that the power of the Spirit is made manifest in action: hatred is melted by the fire of God's powerful love; grief and loss are eased through the power of consolation often mediated through the Christian community; wounds of alienation are soothed by the oil of compassion. The Spirit of God is working at every moment comforting us in our sorrows and challenging us to new levels of conversion.

Biblical images capture the power of the Spirit: Pentecostal *fire* that enflames the lives of the disciples; Pentecostal *wind* that stirs up and blows away the debris that tends to clutter our lives; Pentecostal *light* that empowers us to see the values that tell of the kingdom of God. Human experiences instruct us well that fire, wind and light can aid our lives or destroy them. Through these symbols we have a comparison so that we might better understand the working of the Spirit in our lives.

The power of the Holy Spirit is evidenced throughout Christian history: St. Paul experienced God's power on the road to Damascus; St. Augustine tasted the light of God's brightness under a tree as he pondered scripture; St. Thomas More knew the power of courage as he laid down his life for his faith. We need not go back centuries to record the action and power of the Spirit—our own days provide documentation. The teacher imparting insight, the parent showing gentleness, the priest proclaiming the word of God with enthusiasm, the haunting spring evening filled with a subtle presence. Our faith interprets such events as the working of God in time and space.

There is a paradox here however. Often we experience not power but powerlessness on the journey of life. Weakness can almost dominate our lives. At times we wonder whether or not the Spirit of God's power is operative at all. Here emerges the paradox: when we are weak, then we are strong. St. Paul narrates this experience in faltering words. It was precisely in those moments when he was empty of his own personal resources that room was created for the presence of the Spirit. Jesus too emptied himself and it was in this "powerlessness" that he triumphed. A strange glory here.

The Christian perspective turns everything upside down. We interpret power in a way very different from politicians, economists and military personnel. The power of grace is nothing other than love. Any other type of power must be carefully and critically exercised. Graham Greene entitled one of his books *The Power And The Glory*. In it we discover that God's power is made manifest in the weakness of human nature.

REUNION

There is no better way for us
To come together, you and I,
To stand before this altar, heads
Upturned to lights and images,
To wine and bread, those signs of life
And growth. There is no better way
To look upon each other and affirm
Your mystery and my mystery, your
Uprising youth and my unbending
Age, to speak to you from my center
To your center while the liturgy
Of resurrection rears around us
And we stand as we shall stand
Before we mount together the mystic stairs.

Brother Edward Seifert, F.S.C.

Mission Impossible

There are comfort zones in our life and the challenge to move out of them can be extremely distressing. Yet that is exactly what we are called to in our Christian faith: to be sent by the Lord into the lives of others in service. This means that we must often leave behind our own interests and "comforts" so as to be agents of the Lord's love and concern. Being sent is mission. Being sent is to be given a task to accomplish in the building of the kingdom.

Is this mission possible? The once popular TV program *Mission Impossible* presented the chief characters pulling off extraordinary feats with considerable ease—and week after week. One would think that eventually they would fail. By way of comparison the mission we have as Christians seems to take on the characteristic of impossibility. Is unity really an achievable ideal? Can there really be justice and peace in the world? Are fragile human beings able to transcend their own self-interest in being for and with others? Indeed a mission impossible—without grace and the working of the Spirit. Here truth is stranger than fiction or any television program. The incredible mission of reconciling all creation to the Father is being worked out in subtle ways despite all the apparent obstacles and setbacks.

Basically what is the heart of our mission? To translate gospel values into everyday life. Proclamation is not enough. We must allow the word of God to become incarnate through our lives. In spite of our inadequacy and infidelity, we do on occasion become instruments of God's forgiveness and love, we do grieve with the broken-hearted and forlorn, we do our peacemaking in dangerous situations. Through the gift of the Spirit we are empowered to see what our mission is and to bring it into reality.

The word "mission" is often associated with foreign lands.

Christian people are sent to Central America, Appalachia or Africa in response to God's call. This expression of mission is powerful and clear. But no less powerful is the mission we have at home to reach out to one another, to heal divisions within our family and community, to promote peace and justice in our own nation. Every Christian by definition is missioned. Every Christian is empowered by the Spirit for a unique work.

Henri Nouwen's book *Reaching Out* is an excellent resource for dealing with the spiritual life, that life in which we are called to respond to God's word in community. The title strikes the target at the very center. Mission is to reach out to the abandoned and poor, the isolated and lonely, those who are hurting in any way. Mission can happen at any moment. We extend our hands and hearts to our brothers and sisters. Our mission is to build community. Mission happens when the deed of love is done—with joy!

COMMUNITY

This country
       is patch-work quilt
     when seen from sky beyond,
       high above fog
           and other cloaking things
that try to hide
       beauty below.
One willing to look,
           however,
will view wonders undreamable—
       land too vast to imagine—
towns, cities
       carefully laid out
   to benefit *all* people,
       not just builders—
greenery in places
       never before expected,
on trees, as grass on ground,
       in numerous fields
already plowed under
           if up North.
       How can a land
       this huge
not have room?

                                  Barbara J. Holt

Spitballers Beware

Justice is about people. When the right to life, the right to respect, the right to freedom, the right to an education, the basic right to human dignity are all protected and promoted then justice is being worked out. In the real world there is something else at work: injustice. Prejudices, biases, discrimination, exploitation—these forces reek of alienation, pain and even death. The Church clearly states that there is no peace without justice; there is no peace either within or outside the Church unless every person is dealt with in a reverent and respectful way.

Years ago our grade school class was detained after school hours because of some spitballs that had been inappropriately hurled during a time of "intense learning." These distracting missiles evoked no small anger in our teacher. She rendered judgment: no one would leave the room until the criminal came forward with a full confession. The spitballer (who goes unnamed) hid behind the silence. The class was indignant that one hostile adult could perpetrate such injustice on a whole class. We might laugh at such a situation but we do not laugh at the injustice that rages throughout the world: people locked in prison without due process; individuals barred from educational and political processes because of race; gifted people unable to share their talents because of autocratic leadership. Wherever injustice reigns the kingdom is threatened.

Justice is more than a theory. Justice demands action that flows from commitment and courage. The Spirit of the Lord is given to us so that we might fulfill our duties and obligations so clearly articulated in scripture. The Spirit helps us to overcome our fears and gives us the courage to act in the face of suffering and even death. Without the Spirit we are powerless and blind, not even realizing the injustices within our systems and within our own persons.

Micah, the Old Testament prophet, captures much of God's will in stating: "This is what Yahweh is asking of you, only this—to act justly, to love tenderly, to walk humbly with your God." Biblical commands are not given without the necessary grace to accomplish them. It is the Spirit that empowers us to do the mission of Jesus. It is the Spirit of justice, love and faith that leads to the doing of the Father's will.

Biblical justice reaches far beyond the Greek concept of justice. The justice of God finds its heart in mercy and love. Yet, in the name of mercy or love, we cannot allow a strict, unfeeling and legalistic justice to go on unchecked. History has too many examples of people unwilling to change unjust systems because it seemed more "loving" to stay with the *status quo*. This is a cop-out. Love without justice is not authentic. Again the Spirit empowers us to discern the expression and form of both love and justice in our lives.

MOTHER TERESA

When Mother Teresa holds a child
She holds a star.
"See what I have picked from the rubble
There on back stairs where the rats were nibbling."
She holds it close as though
This were the one living light
And she must warm her fingers in its beauty.
"See what I have plucked from the pavement,
A star fallen from God's crown.
Do you think, my brothers, my sisters,
That there can be too many stars,
Too many lights on the earth?"

                              Brother Edward Seifert, F.S.C.

One Of These Days

Several months ago I joined some friends on a kayaking expedition. Our basic goal of running the Pine River failed because of a series of obstacles: the trailer carrying our kayaks broke down, the roads to the river turned out to be inaccessible, and we ran out of time because of the first two problems. An event such as this must be simply chalked up as "one of those days." Detours and pitfalls are part of life. Hopefully the next time things will go well and the Pine River will be traveled with joy and delight.

The mission of Jesus faces its own kind of roadblocks. The values and life style that he preached and lived come up against some very strong opposition. It is important that we reflect on what it is that prevents that mission from being accomplished. With this knowledge we can then plan on what we might do to overcome the pitfalls and continue on the journey toward the kingdom. I would like to suggest that three perennial obstacles face individuals and systems: ignorance, fear and apathy.

To achieve any task some knowledge is necessary. Where we are going determines what means are necessary to arrive at the goal. Jesus' mission gradually became clear to his disciples. They had to be led out of *ignorance* into a vision of what the harvest was all about. A sense of mission can be distorted because of jaundiced eyes or false information. At times in history leaders imposed baptism on a conquered people. This practice obviously is not in accord with the mission given to us. A good theology, i.e., a carefully articulated understanding of our faith experience, is important in overcoming the roadblock of ignorance. We have a duty to study and reflect upon God's word and presence in our lives.

Fear can also prevent the realization of a mission. One of the greatest obstacles for a person going back to school after being out for ten or more years is apprehension: will I be able to concentrate long enough to comprehend the required assignments? The mission of Jesus can also instill fear in the human heart. With that mission comes suffering and pain as well as joy and consolation. With that mission comes the call to die to self in order that life may be given to us. Death causes us to tremble. The mission of Jesus thrusts us into the world of forgiveness and love. Indeed the price tag for discipleship is very high and the fear can be very deep.

Mission demands ministry or action. Sometimes we are not willing to move. Inertia sets in and we become extremely comfortable with the way things are. Challenge becomes a threat. Defensively we cry out that we have so many pressing personal needs that we cannot find the time and energy for larger experiences in serving others. Thus we come into contact with a third roadblock: *apathy*. Because of other concerns we are indifferent to the call to be agents of reconciliation and peace, people of justice, persons striving for holiness. Maybe tomorrow or next year I will get involved. Jesus invited the rich young man to follow him but the response was negative.

However, the forces of ignorance, fear and apathy face a much stronger power. The Spirit of knowledge, the Spirit of trust and the Spirit of commitment has been given to us. Jesus and the Father send their Spirit into our lives that we might overcome every detour on the pilgrimage. With such help and power the journey can be made with courage and joy.

SPIRIT OF TRUTH

But when the Spirit of truth comes,
He will lead you to the complete truth—John 16:13

God moves in wondrous ways—
In morning manna, wine from water,
Bread that tumbles out of baskets—
And now, beyond surmise,
In shuffled papers, chalkboard scrawl,
Loosed tongues at summer workshop.

It must have been the spirit that sat
(Exotic bird,
Unruffled bird of passage)
As we went stumbling over paradigms
Of love and prayer and action.

In wondrous ways, even at long tables
Littered with our notes and wavering outlines
Spirit moves.
From eye to eye, from lip to lip
The wonder grew
And it was Pentecost in midsummer.

Brother Edward Seifert, F.S.C.

No Utopian Camelot

The word "utopia" refers to an ideal situation. A utopian society is one in which there are no conflicts or tensions, no injustices or hatred, no wars or violence. It is important to note that etymologically the word "utopia" means "no place." As much as we desire a Camelot, it simply does not exist—at least not on planet Earth.

Through baptism and the other sacraments we are continually being empowered with the gift of the Holy Spirit. One might begin to expect, with a loving God dwelling in the Church and in our hearts, that life should be without struggle. Yet tensions and conflicts remain in our lives. Although we are offered a graced life, there are always sinful areas of our minds and hearts—both within ourselves and our society. No matter what chronological age we have reached or what degree of psychological maturity, conversion will be a process moving us from darkness to light, from selfishness to love, from sin to grace. Conversion means that throughout the pilgrimage certain tensions will have to be dealt with.

One tension facing all of us is that between legitimate self-interest and the call to reach out to others. In making decisions as to how we will use our limited time and energy, there is a twofold demand: to attend to my own needs and to attend to those of the larger religious and civic societies. Resolution is not easy. The stresses and strains caused by a variety of demands and societal expectations foster frustration. At times balance is lost and we venture off either to radical self-interest or to involvements that exceed our capacities. Either choice is injurious to holistic health. We need the Spirit of discernment to maintain a prudent balance.

The demands of prayer and action can also be a source of tension for many. Ideally our ministry flows out of a prayer life. Yet, in the real situation, activism can exclude quiet time with the Lord Jesus as personal prayer can become egocentric when it does not deepen our life of charity. In one of his novels Graham Greene makes this observation regarding one of the characters: ". . . prayer demanded an act and he had no intention of acting." A constant challenge will be to find space for communicating with the Lord while also being willing to take the word he speaks to us and live it in our relationships with our brothers and sisters.

Freedom and authority! Competition or completion? A third tension that occupies much time is the double assertion that we are called to a healthy self-reliance while at the same time we are called to follow legitimate authority. This is true in the home, in civic society and in the Church. Throughout history we witness much confusion regarding the exercise of freedom for those who are in positions of power. Again the danger is to opt for an either/or solution rather than a both/and. The Spirit calls us to a radical freedom and to obedience in the same breath. We must constantly pray for the grace to sort this out.

Would that our planet and human existence were less messy. Would that utopia could be found (as some claim it has in the NW corner of Outagamie County). At times the stresses and strains will be too much and polarities will set in. Eccentric behavior happens because of egocentric attitudes. Each day we must pray: "Veni Creator Spiritus." Come, Holy Spirit! With the coming of the Spirit we have a chance of keeping our balance.

BALANCE

So what is one to do,
   when mind whirls
      like devilish dervish
around worry of work
   not meeting other's standards
while exceeding one's own—
   when looked at in perspective
         and alone,
away from perfectionist expectations
   or outlandish demands
never quite down to earth
      when viewed from afar.
Is door
      to another world
         now ajar?
Is it possible,
      feasible,
      now,
that spirit and soul
      shall move on
to search for those
         like minded and
knowing good
      when it is seen?

Barbara J. Holt

DISCIPLESHIP

R.S.V.P.

A priest friend of mine, working in the mountains northeast of Lima, Peru, wrote to me telling me of his work. Circumstances were not favorable: weeks of rain had caused numerous mud slides throughout his parish; few people were available to proclaim and teach the gospel; rampant poverty deprived his people of proper shelter and food.

Yet, his letter went on to say, the people had deep joy and loving hearts. Though the suffering was great, their faith was strong and enduring. Putting the letter aside, I paused to try and capture the tone of this letter. One word came to mind: *discipleship.*

Jesus came to be with people in need; he came to share the Father's love and forgiveness. He also came to call others to carry on this mission of reconciling all creation to his Father.

In that invitation to discipleship people were challenged to leave behind certain values and ways of life for the sake of the kingdom—God's kingdom of peace, truth, love, freedom and justice.

The disciple, responding to the Lord's call, replaces hatred with love, vengeance with forgiveness, selfishness with commitment. The call that Jesus gave in biblical times echoes through the ages. All of us, regardless of our state in life, are invited to discipleship through our baptismal call.

Christian discipleship contains the grace of friendship. Jesus says to the disciples: "I no longer call you servants, but friends." The invitation to friendship with Christ involves a commitment to life, whatever the cost. Friendship implies kindred spirits—seeing the same things, rejoicing in the same values, desiring the same goals. Discipleship draws us into the community of believers.

A twentieth century political and religious leader, Mahatma Gandhi, attracted many disciples because of his commitment to truth and justice, freedom and love. People saw in Gandhi's nonviolent life style an ideal that respected the dignity of the human person and an ideal that allowed all persons to maintain their own integrity. A model was observable; the ideal was not only attainable but lived.

In faith we know that Jesus is the master and Lord of all creation. Like a magnet he draws us into his presence, offering us his wisdom and power. Discipleship is to align ourselves with his conviction and to live his commitment.

Invitations need not be answered. Yet if we look carefully, at the bottom of every page of scripture are the initials R.S.V.P. Busy about many things we can miss the one thing that is necessary: to make our lives an act of love. Discipleship demands a basic simplicity. We are to cut through whatever is peripheral and accidental and come to the heart of the matter. God is love and we are made to his image and likeness.

Discipleship focuses upon this call and realizes that everything else is secondary. We cannot have many masters; we cannot respond to contradictory value systems in life. A free and loving choice must be made to allow the Lord to be Lord of our lives—thus we become disciple/friend.

My friend in Lima responded to the invitation to discipleship and went to the missions. A teacher, sharing truth in the classroom, is a disciple with a great mission. Parents, loving each other and their children into the fullness of life, have heard the call of concern and become disciples. Discipleship embraces every walk of life.

The Lord's invitation extends from one end of the earth to the other—and hopefully that invitation will receive an affirmative response.

THE CALL

Caw! Caw! Caw!
    God spoke again this morning
        through a morning crow celebrating spring
        through raisin bran sustaining life
        through a psalm singing hope.

Yes! Yes! Yes!
    God spoke years ago,
        through a parent's faith-filled life
        through a teacher's spirit-guided love
        through a priest's inviting demand.

Holy! Holy! Holy!
    God speaks forever now
        through roses, His thorned-filled love unfolding
        through smiles, His laughter exploding
        through pain, His cross sharing.

                        Robert F. Morneau

The Lone Ranger Is Dead

Back in the 1940's a popular hero for many grade school children (and perhaps not a few adults) was the Lone Ranger. In fact for just 25 cents and a boxtop you could order a ring with a silver bullet attached in which you could put secret messages. What more could a person ask for?

Unfortunately this model of working alone against injustice and evil infected our notion of discipleship. The disciple was separated out "from the world" and was to achieve certain goals without the help of others.

Today the Lone Ranger model is dead. The disciple works in community and recognizes a need for community. People need people. And mutual support and cooperation are necessary for the full life of the Church.

To understand the life of the disciple in community let us address three tensions present in it: the experience of consolation and challenge; the pull between the *I* and the *We*; and the need for solitude and involvement. By avoiding the either/or option, a healthy balance can be attained.

Consolation/Challenge. A great gift in life is the consoling word or touch. Life has many difficulties and anxieties; blessed is the person who is surrounded by people who offer to help in carrying its burdens.

The disciple of Jesus needs both to give and to receive this precious pearl; the disciple of Jesus needs community. But community also brings confrontation and conflict. Insensitivities, misunderstanding or simple selfishness will create tensions that must be addressed.

Discipleship demands that we confront sin in others as well as be confronted ourselves when we have sinned by causing division and alienation. Community provides the atmosphere and setting for consolation and challenge, key activities in the conversion and growth process for every Christian.

I/We. Throughout history the human community has been challenged to hold in delicate balance the dignity of the individual while at the same time giving full value to the social side of human nature. The disciple feels keenly the pull between providing for individual needs and reaching out to the common good.

But the disciple is not alone in the discernment process. The community has an obligation to call the disciple to take time off for proper recreation and relaxation; it also has the obligation to hold the disciple responsible for essential duties. On the other side of the coin the disciple challenges the community to move from parochialism to a sense of the solidarity of the world, all people being part of God's single family.

Historically the balance has not been well kept. Oftentimes there is a swing into a radical individualism, at other times, into an unhealthy collectivism. Discipleship must confront this danger and, in grace, seek to make decisions that protect both the well-being of society *and* the rights of each individual.

Solitude/Involvement. Human growth takes place only when there is sufficient space and time to be in touch with the Source of our being. A life of complete activism kills the spirit. Human growth also demands sharing our giftedness with others in generous service. The community must provide its leaders with quiet time so that the inner agenda may be adequately dealt with.

The community also calls its members to recognize, develop and express their giftedness in constructive ways. The pendulum tends to swing either to a type of quietism which fails to appreciate social involvement or, perhaps more commonly in our times, into a powerful activism which excludes those quiet moments where we can rest in the presence of our God.

Perhaps the Lone Ranger is not dead, at least the tendency to go it alone. But to allow ourselves to be cut off from community, to become marginal, is devastating and discipleship cannot afford this. Jesus went out for the one sheep knowing that alone it would not survive and alone it could not contribute to the flock. Discipleship and community must exist together or both die.

NARROW DOOR

My key chain is lost, Lord,
How do I get in?
Knuckles sore from knocking,
Feet from sin.

There is the key of truth, Lord,
And freedom, justice and love.
Will these pry open the narrow door,
To the giant feast of love?

Robert F. Morneau

A Vitamin A Day Keeps . . .

Last summer I was gone for a week and forgot to have someone tend the flowers in my room. When I returned home, I sensed a certain indignation coming through the drooping leaves: "Could you not have found someone to tend to us during your absence?"

Discipleship is not unlike a plant that must be nourished and carefully tended. Survival and growth are not automatic. Certain nutrients must be present if the heart of discipleship, our relationship with Christ, is to be maintained.

Our Catholic tradition provides rich fare here. The Eucharist, prayer and scripture are central graces that keep our life in Christ alive and flourishing.

Gathering at the Lord's table to celebrate the mystery of God's love and forgiveness is a most powerful grace. The fathers of Vatican Council II tell us that "the liturgy is the summit toward which the activity of the Church is directed; at the same time it is the fountain from which all her power flows."

Here the word of God enlightens the mind and enflames the heart of the disciple; here the body of Jesus is given for our salvation; here we are sent forth to share the love and forgiveness received with the rest of the world.

Nourishment takes place at every level: physical, psychological and spiritual. Disciples bring their lives to the liturgy and they take the grace of the liturgy back into life. There can be no separation of life and liturgy as if they were two totally distinct tracks we are to walk. No disciple can afford to neglect the Eucharist, the fountain and source of nourishment for our spiritual lives.

The quality of any relationship is determined by the quality of communication. Discipleship is friendship with the Lord and the communication process that gives quality to that relationship is called prayer: a listening and responding in reverent mutuality. Because of the many demands on the lives of today's disciples prayer is threatened.

"My life is my prayer"—"my ministry is my prayer" are not unpopular mottoes. Ministry is indeed a major means of sanctification but how long it can be sustained without personal prayer is a serious question. Discipleship demands prayer and that means there will be need for silence, solitude and surrender.

The disciple is a scriptural person. Both the Hebrew scriptures and the New Testament provide a vision of the meaning of life and the workings of our gracious God.

In the Bible we find the reflections of faith communities as they interpret how God has broken into history with his redeeming love. The psalmist shares prayers of deep personal experience; the prophets call people to a renewal of their ideals and to fidelity; the gospels proclaim the tremendous love and forgiveness of God in Jesus and through the Spirit; the letters of St. Paul describe the early communities and give the message that he felt compelled to preach—the message of Jesus crucified.

The story of scripture is our story. As we read our past, our future is unfolding in our hearts. As disciples we must be in touch with God's word on a daily basis. For without scripture, we are lost on an ocean without a compass.

The nutrients for growth in discipleship range far beyond Eucharist, prayer and scripture. Personal friends, spiritual writers, daily encounters with fellow pilgrims, subtle intuitions of the heart are other channels whereby God's gracious touch can be felt in our lives. Yet these three ingredients of liturgy, scripture and quiet communication with God are extremely significant and central.

A primary obligation for all of us is to go to these fountains and to drink deeply. And in the drinking our personal nourishment will overflow in a ministry that is grounded in a rich interiority.

PRAYER

It is so easy
To write about prayer,
Like writing smooth songs
About rain in your hair.
Words come from ambience
Of midsummer rose,
Light as your breathing
In midday repose.

But once I have written
And laid words aside,
I enter the prayer gate
Beckoning wide.
I stand on the causeway
Frail and alone
And I feel my way
Through tunneling stone.

I stumble and lean for support
Against fog-wet walls.
This place I called holy
Chills and appalls.
It was so simple
To write about prayer,
I thought as the Nameless
Fronted me there.

Edward Seifert, F.S.C.

How Much Does It Cost?

It seems strange that an economic term—*cost*—would be used in talking about a religious commitment. Yet anyone who enters into the life of Jesus comes to know very quickly that a price is demanded, the price of dying to self over and over again in a variety of ways.

The mystery of the cross brings into sharp focus the very essence of discipleship which is the price that is exacted in participating fully in the life of Jesus.

Many people courageously and generously pay the price of discipleship: the parent who refuses to give up on a prodigal child; the child who continues to struggle to love an alcoholic parent; the politician who confronts injustice and strives to change oppressive systems, even if it means endangering one's office; the artist who attempts to give birth to beauty and truth; the hospital chaplain who enters into the tragedies of the suffering; the first grade teacher who spends countless hours helping the little people learn to read and write; the terminally ill who embrace their lot with nobility; the youth who faces ridicule and sarcasm in living out a Christian value system. Who can measure the price that is paid for such integrity and honesty?

By following the path marked out by Christ, the cross leads us into the glory and victory of the resurrection.

A disciple is one who has the ability and willingness to experience pain with people. Instinctively most of us tend to turn away from pain or even flee from it. Grace is needed if we are to enter into the sufferings of life and find God's grace in these vulnerable moments.

A case could well be made for the adage "patior ergo sum" (I suffer; therefore I am). This is not to be sadistic. Rather some of the deepest and most meaningful experiences of human life are to be found precisely in the center of great suffering.

Facades are broken down, life is tasted to the full. A disciple of Jesus is fully alive and fully human because life is experienced in its depths. Catherine of Siena once wrote about Jesus' response to her regarding the question of suffering: ". . . she suffers because she loves Me, nor would she suffer if she did not love Me."

Herein lies a great mystery. Discipleship is able to embrace suffering because the love is great. Like all relationships—be they between God and a person, husband and wife, friend and friend—there will be days of joy and pain. What is constant is the presence of love and it is this grace that sustains relationships regardless of what happens.

Nobody wants to suffer. Affliction is not appealing to the human heart. It should not be surprising that few actually follow the way of Christ though many profess to walk his road. Even the apostles tried to deter Jesus from going up to Jerusalem. Jesus had to be very stern with Peter in rebuking him for buying into human standards and not those of his Father.

Thus our struggle is not uncommon. Would that we could walk around the cross and join in Christ's resurrection in some other way than dying.

Another economic term comes to mind: *payoff*. It may seem crass and yet, for anyone who is willing to enter into the cost of discipleship, there is a trade-off—the victory over sin and death. By giving ourselves in love and service, a peace comes into our lives that cannot be described.

This is the promise that our Lord made to all who enter into his service—the promise of peace and eternal life. Cost and payoff, death and resurrection, suffering and peace. The disciple is not afraid to live in the land of paradox and mystery.

THE COST OF DISCIPLESHIP

Life goes on,
        despite pains of some
who have lost all
        meaning for their world
when love and soul
        have gone,
leaving behind only
                emptiness
so deep
        it hurts to even cry
        for it,
and life continues on,
    sailing by
        smiling hearts
letting worries slide off
    carefree but caring shoulders,
supporting self
            and others
        with bottomless wellspring
            bubbling up strength
and courage
to not let
        negative
            triumph.

                                        Barbara J. Holt

Scars Revisited

One evening on a retreat experience some years ago, a special session was held that dealt with healing, the healing of memories. During the prayer service the participants were asked to reverently reflect upon their life journey going back as far as they could remember.

As their life was reviewed, they were asked to get in touch with the hurts and pain that they had either caused or received. The purpose was to take each moment of suffering and give it to the Lord for healing, for forgiveness. Tears of sorrow and tears of joy were shed.

As disciples of Jesus Christ we come to recognize that oftentimes we need healing. Old hurts, past resentments, scars that have not yet been adequately dealt with can take a lot of energy away from us that could be used for more constructive purposes.

Once they are given to the Lord, we are much freer in his service. Healing of memories can be a powerful enriching experience, however painful.

It may well be that our effectiveness as disciples of the Lord is somewhat proportionate to the experience of healing in our lives. To the extent that we are open to reconciliation that comes to us through the sacraments and community, to that degree will we have compassion to understand the pain of others.

The eyes of the disciple say a lot—they say whether or not the disciple has walked through the valley of heartache and suffering. Indeed we are all wounded healers. We cannot afford to be out of touch with the universal experience of suffering, lest we become insensitive and hard of heart.

The healing of disciples is not limited to memories. In the present moment perhaps our hearts need to be healed of coldness and indifference; our minds may need the Lord's forgiving touch because of some darkness and confusion; our hands, lacking enthusiasm, need to be strengthened to reach out and assist others; our imaginations need healing if our dreams are to be holy, our visions clear; our communities need divine compassion because of narrowness and apathy; our planet earth, weak and fragile, needs healing because of the human exploitation that has battered and bruised it so severely.

In calling us to be disciples, Jesus asks us to continue his work. He came not for people who are well and have it all put together; rather, he came for those who are ill and lost that he might bring them back to the Father. We identify with this ministry only after recognizing and being grateful for the fact that the Lord continues to come into our own lives to restore our health.

When we heal and reconcile others, we are also healed and reconciled. At times this position can be rather uncomfortable: when we think, perhaps, that we have already arrived, or should have arrived, at fullness of health. This simply is not the situation.

Flannery O'Connor, a great fiction writer, once wrote to a friend: "In a sense sickness is a place, more instructive than a long trip to Europe, and it's always a place where there's no company, where nobody can follow. Sickness before death is a very appropriate thing and I think those who don't have it miss one of God's mercies."

She wrote this at a time when she was suffering from the severe illness which eventually took her life. In deep faith, O'Connnor came to see the meaning of suffering and even to label it a mercy. Her Christian vocation to be a writer was, for her, one of discipleship. Although not healed of body, she was healed in spirit, and in that grace she expressed thanks.

THAT THEY MAY BE ONE

Father, may they be one in us
as you are in me and I in you—John 17:21

Like a melodic refrain the words run
Over the earth. The prayer at the covenant table
Peals in soft bell tones over the living.
That they may be one, he prays
Over the steppe, the plain, and the hill
And man-filled valleys and deltas under the moon.
That they may be one, he prays
Over crescent and cross, over altar and fire,
Over children and men who cry
To a Father they somehow see through their tears.

They are already one in his vision
As he prays for perfection in knowing
And completeness in loving,
One in his vision as at the world's center
He prays, his Father beside him.

                                        Edward Seifert, F.S.C.

Taking The Stand

In his powerful autobiography entitled *Witness*, Whittaker Chambers describes how he broke from being a communist and lived out a different value system. He felt compelled to share his story with his children and anyone else interested in his human and often tortuous journey. Because of his witness, many lives have been affected.

A key function of the community of disciples that gather around Jesus is to witness to our contemporary world a set of values and a vision that challenges the present options. An alternative is given to our highly materialistic and consumeristic culture. Witnessing and taking a prophetic stance helps to proclaim what is near and dear to our hearts.

Discipleship has a mission: to bring to a weary world the values of love, forgiveness, compassion, healing. Christ continues to live in and act through his disciples. The challenge is to be fitting instruments in cooperating with the mission that Jesus had.

One model of the Church today is that of being a herald and prophet. Prophets are people who proclaim vigorously and with zeal the vision of the Lord. They are willing to confront any value system that denies or contradicts the gospels. Indeed this part of the prophetic role is not pleasant.

Not surprisingly, many who are called to this task have strong resistance. Yet the work must be done and the warning must be spoken. Another dimension of the prophet's task is to provide hope. An alternative life style is presented and the possibility of living it out is given. Ultimately the prophet is a life-giver and a bringer of hope.

What is crucial in the life of the disciple/prophet is life style. Only so far as our manner of life is congruent with the life of Jesus will we be found to be credible and authentic. Unless the disciple actually follows the Lord in obedience, simplicity and love, there will be no impact on the world. Rather scandal will result because people see the gap between what is proclaimed and how the proclaimer lives.

Discipleship is more than a function or task; it is a way of life. Thus the notion of "mission," of being sent, is powerful and exact. We are sent, like Jesus, to *be* a type of presence in the world today. To *do* comes after and, though significant, it is always secondary.

Our identity is wrapped up in the fact that Jesus is Lord and master. Such a discipleship demands commitment, loyalty and sacrifice. Its center is vibrant because it is filled with love. Our challenge will always be to incarnate God's love and forgiveness in time and space. Our mission will be that of Jesus: to proclaim a year of favor, to heal the broken-hearted, to free the oppressed. No greater task can be given a person.

Is discipleship only a dream or is it truly possible? Our eyes are set on the Lord and we know the road he walked—and we know of many others who faithfully stayed with him. Our ultimate task is one of fidelity—remaining faithful to the gift of the Spirit that empowers us to live the Christian life.

We do not travel alone. And so the words of mission continue to ring in our ears:

"Go, therefore, make disciples of all the nations; baptize them in the name of the Father and of the Son and of the Holy Spirit, and teach them to observe all the commands I gave you. And know that I am with you always; yes, to the end of time" (Mt 28:19-20).

WITNESS AND MISSION

Perhaps this year
  celebration of Holy Week
will come
  in seeing self
    as wholly weak,
in need of salvation
    and of friends,
    of quiet walks
      or silent talks with
        God within,
without negative paths—
    already so deeply entrenched
    in scattered brain—
being crossed over
    and over again.
One crucifixion
  is enough
    for any man
or woman—

                              Barbara J. Holt

EVANGELIZATION

The Infection Of Faith

Recently I received from a friend a cassette tape containing the music of a jazz pianist by the name of George Winston. As I listened to the delightful sound the music worked its way into my heart. Soon after, I found myself spontaneously buying copies of the tape to give to friends. Although out several dollars, I knew that the joy I experienced would now become part of the lives of those I loved.

Evangelization, as a process of sharing, follows the same pattern described above. We encounter the person of Jesus Christ in the Church, in the sacraments, in personal prayer; we allow him to enter our hearts and dwell there; we experience his tender love and consoling forgiveness; we then share our faith with others. Key to the whole process is ACCEPTANCE: the Lord is the one to whom we give our allegiance. Often this means a "change of lords"—giving up certain behavioral patterns or even relationships that are incompatible with gospel values. If the acceptance is authentic and deep, we will be moved to share the good news we have received with others. Keeping a secret is difficult. Meeting someone who loves us and shares life deeply also lends itself to sharing. Good news bursts beyond our narrow selves to touch the lives of others.

A former professor of philosophy passed on an old adage: goodness is diffusive of itself. I struggled to understand this pithy axiom. An example was helpful: a loving smile tends to draw a smile out of others in return. A good deed creates an atmosphere which elicits other kind responses. Goodness is infectious; faith tends to create a happy contagion. All this is part of the evangelization process. The experience of Jesus as Lord, once accepted, has its own dynamism and movement.

The problem consistently has been rejection—so many walked away from Jesus because they found his message too difficult or simply did not understand.

The gift of faith demands a life of sacrifice and self-giving. Albert Nolan, in his provocative study *Jesus before Christianity*, writes: "In the last analysis faith is not a way of speaking or a way of thinking, it is a way of living and can only be adequately articulated in a living praxis. To acknowledge Jesus as our Lord and Savior is only meaningful insofar as we try to live as he lived and to order our lives according to his values" (Maryknoll, NY: Orbis Books, 1978, p. 139). Acceptance means a change of life style; it means entering into a process of ongoing conversion. Acceptance can be tested by the way we live. What characterized the life of Jesus was obedience to the Father's will and self-giving for others. No surprise then to see many walk away from such an invitation.

The title of evangelist is not all that familiar within our Catholic tradition. Few people would claim that because of their baptism they are necessarily evangelists. Yet that is what we are called to be. Acceptance of Jesus as Lord implies a willingness to share the gift of his friendship that we have received. Such evangelization is not necessarily one that involves formal preaching or even teaching. Yet we proclaim by our very lives and our personality who we are and what we believe. Through the proclamation of our values and attitudes we either lead people toward God or away from him. Acceptance of the Lord must be followed by sharing him. Acceptance and evangelization are of one piece.

ACCEPTANCE

God's people
    say good night
Creaky cricket
    chirps unsteady stutters—
    heat's not high enough
    for constant song.
Rabbits rustle dry grass
    as they hop from supper
        to snack and back again.
Belated June bug
    mimics melody
      long gone
    with rest of summer's story.
Good night to you, too,
      God's good people.

Barbara J. Holt

Will It Fly?

In December, 1903, the Wright brothers went to the windswept sand dunes of Kitty Hawk, North Carolina, to see whether or not their aircraft would fly. Legend has passed down the phrase: "It won't fly, Orville!" Well, the truth of the matter proved otherwise. The plane flew, the dream was realized. Aviation was born and it has revolutionized the world.

In an age when cultural despair and a sense of fatalism is strong, the question arises as to whether or not the good news of salvation still "flies." Does the message of God's love and forgiveness in Jesus influence the mind and hearts of twentieth century persons? A central task of evangelization is to get the message off the launch pad. The blueprint of God's word and loving design must find expression in history. Our personal relationships, social concerns and internalized values are vehicles through which the evangelizing process is lived out. The hallmarks of authentic and credible Christian living are the quality of our love, the depth of our faith, and the inclusiveness of our compassion.

Authentic and credible evangelization could take the shape of a food pantry organized to feed the hungry and destitute; a scripture scholar's spending countless hours going over texts so as to communicate more accurately the word of God; the hand of forgiveness extended to someone who has done us wrong; a person kneeling in silence to pray to God in thanksgiving, praise, petition; counselors and spiritual directors being available to those who need to share their journey of joy and sorrow. Evangelization is not an abstract reality. It is something we do every day by taking the good news of salvation and enfleshing it through love, forgiveness and concern.

There is a pragmatic side to evangelization. Change takes place when gospel values are lived out. The very presence of

Jesus liberates; the very word of God contains great power. Ultimately evangelization flows from and instills a sense of hope. Things can be different; there are new possibilities; a sense of freshness is in the air. The Spirit provides an energy that transforms our darkness into light, our discouragement into zeal, our doubt into faith. When values are lived, then people begin to realize that the promise made by God is not just an ideal but already has taken on substance. Evangelization is confirmed by the practice of our faith.

Will it fly? We need not ask Orville or anyone else. Evangelization will get off the launch pad and make its flight only if it is a response to God's word as it touches our individual and communal lives. The initiative is with God but our cooperation is of great importance. As disciples of Jesus we are given the privilege of sharing with others the good news that we have received. As brothers and sisters of a common Father, we are challenged to share the goods of which we are simply stewards. As immortal diamonds we are true to our dignity by letting the grace of God shine through our lived experience. When this happens the success of the Wright brothers will pale in comparison to the witness that we offer.

SIMON'S HOUSE

No water—no kiss—no oil.
A strange house this.
The invitation seemed warm enough
Perhaps I failed to smile.

But his love is small,
Though table and friends large.
A strange house this.
Where the uninvited—bear the gift of bliss.

Robert F. Morneau

Once Upon A Time

Storytelling is a fascinating art. Almost everyone is trapped with the words: "Once upon a time. . . ." In stories we meet people (from Snow White to Captain Ahab), we feel strong emotions (from ecstasy to despair), we get caught up into action (from receptive wonder to violent struggle). Some stories are tragic, some comic; others are filled with joy, some with deep suffering; many stories are ordinary, a few incredibly spellbinding. But then there is our story which perhaps embraces elements of all of these above.

As Christians we live a faith story, i.e., a story in which God plays a most significant role. Not only is God our creator but we believe, in faith, that he continues to be with us through his caring love and challenging word. But is our faith story ever told? Do we share with others in community how God works (and doesn't work) in our personal lives? This can be most uncomfortable for a variety of reasons. For some of us, perhaps, our faith life is primarily individual and private, something we simply don't talk about. For others, our own story may not seem to be that terribly interesting to warrant taking someone else's time for a friendly sharing. Still for others, God talk sounds "pious" and might be offensive to secular ears. Or we may not be all that sensitive to God's inner workings and thus don't know what to say, how to say it, or feel there is nothing to be said.

The RENEW program has dispelled many of these obstacles for a number of people and now faith sharing is happening in powerful and dynamic ways. People tell of how God blessed them in terms of a new friendship recently experienced; a destructive life pattern is broken through God's grace and gratitude is expressed and shared; a sin is clearly seen and confessed and the newly won freedom cannot be kept secret. In the very telling of the story, the listeners are influenced and transformed. Further, by means of sharing, others are "freed-up" to communicate deeper aspects of their own lives. Faith sharing has a ripple effect; the faith pebble dropped and shared reaches distant shores.

Storytelling and evangelization go hand in hand. Pope Paul VI wrote:

> Evangelization, as we have said, is a complex process made up of varied elements; the renewal of humanity, witness, explicit proclamation, inner adherence, entry into the community, acceptance of signs, apostolic initiative. These elements may appear to be contradictory, indeed mutually exclusive. In fact they are complementary and mutually enriching. (Evangelii Nuntiandi, #19)

The witnessing element of evangelization is a component of storytelling. We personally and directly invite others into our lives as we narrate our faith experiences. But our stories, though unique, also have a universal quality about them—in some way, all our stories have great similarity. So as God extends to us his love and forgiveness, that very same grace is also offered to others. Our interpretation of how God works in our daily encounters might well serve as an insight for others in their personal understanding of their own journey. Evangelization helps us to see history in depth, from a faith point of view.

Where does our storytelling achieve its greatest focus? Our Catholic tradition is rich in symbolism and ritual. In the sacraments we retell and re-experience how God has and is breaking into our lives. At liturgy we gather around the altar as a people to share the journey of faith. The climax of the story is Eucharist, the mystery of Jesus' self-giving and obedience. His story must become ours; his story must then be shared in word and in the testimony of our lives.

Once upon a time . . . once upon an eternity there was a God extravagantly in love with his people. That is not simply past event, it is a now reality. The good news must be shared, lest we forget the original love story and fail to live it.

THREE MEN

Three men are resting at nightfall,
Each of them spaced from the other
By a hundred miles and twenty.
One has been reading his eyes out
From noon to lamplit dusk.
One has been touching the lonely
In visits on squalid streets,
And the third has been carving out poems
In the glacial life he lives in.
Three men rest and remember
In the nave of churchlike night
And they somehow meet, fingers to fingers,
Heart to heart, as they sit there.
Their fingers are wired, and messages
Run across acres of darkness.
The messages race across cities
And they know, these men at nightfall,
Mystery and communion.

Brother Edward Seifert, F.S.C.

There's Room In the Inn

No trespassing! We have all seen the sign indicating that certain pieces of property are not open to the general public. Hunters are prohibited from a certain woods; snowmobilers, from the golf course; swimmers, from a quarry. Sad to say, such signs and restrictions are not limited to geographic areas. There are "No Trespassing" signs that exclude people because of race, sex, religious beliefs and practices. Such exclusion we label as discrimination and segregation.

The WELCOME mat lies at the base of our doors and hopefully at the entrance of our hearts. We are strangers no more when we become conscious of our solidarity with all people. Our faith reveals to us that God is Father of all; a single family inhabits our small globe. Two characteristics mark out a Christian community: compassion and hospitality. Because we feel deeply with and for others, they gain entrance into our lives. There is, indeed, room in the inn.

But is there? A powerful story from scripture calls us back to reality. Jesus was journeying to Jerusalem. His route took him through a Samaritan town. James and John were sent ahead to secure lodging. This was refused. Immediately the response came: "Lord, would you have us call down fire from heaven to destroy them?" The inhospitality of the Samaritans receives the response of revengeful violence. Jesus rebukes his disciples for such an attitude and misunderstanding of his Father.

The authentic welcome implied in the notion of evangelization has a number of ramifications. One is fidelity. When people enter our faith community we assume a responsibility for and to them; the mutuality of sharing establishes a commitment of deep significance. A second consequence is that our schedules, if not our various houses, will probably be disrupted. Time must be given to nurture relationships established by a gracious welcome. Adaptation and flexibility are not always easy. A third ramification is that welcomes are sometimes refused and the experience of rejection/failure is not uncommon. Feelings of guilt and anxiety may have to be dealt with at these times. Given these possible effects of welcoming people into our community we come to see that such an activity is not romantic. Yet, when it is authentic and a sense of belonging is experienced, the joy is deep—sometimes we call it heaven.

The ultimate goal of evangelization is unity: the oneness of all creation with God. Evangelization is the process that furthers the reconciliation needed in a broken and fragile world. This will not happen without that powerful disposition of hospitality, without that welcoming into the community of those seeking a home. This task falls upon all Christians. It is a style of life: taking initiative when a new person enters a room; inviting the newcomer to join a committee or social group; affirming an idea that leads us to deeper insights; accepting a compliment graciously. Evangelization works its way out in concrete, tangible ways. When people sense that they belong, when they feel one with, then we are fulfilling a primary obligation of the gospel.

My home village is called Bear Creek. It was once named Welcome. I regret the loss of our original name. The larger village of the Church cannot afford to lose its welcome sign that must be printed in bold letters—ALL ARE WELCOME! Our doors must be open or we forfeit the right to claim that we are CATHOLIC!

THE HANDMAID

Mary! a knot untie,
Through a gracious yes.
Unravel twisted, snarled lives,
Binding us to darkness and death.

The sun finds entrance,
Faith scatters the clouds.
Deaths's sickle melts—
Touching an obedient heart's fire.

Servant you are
To redemption's mystery.
Mother are you
To redeemer and redeemed.

Full of grace,
Poor and humble,
Ave, Maria!
Ave.

Robert F. Morneau

Star-Gazing

Our memories can be very slippery. Names are forgotten, appointments are missed, valuable or necessary items are mislaid. Thus strings are sometimes tied around fingers to remind us of important happenings. Problems really begin when we forget to remove the strings once the event has passed. Forgetting can be counteracted by serious and disciplined reflecting. Such reflection is a duty on our faith journey.

Evangelization involves a reflective component that helps us to remember. That reflection involves the use of reason: a serious pondering of questions regarding our identity and destiny. Yet more is involved here. The reflective process of prayer and contemplation is essential if evangelization is to be fully activated. In a subtle way the reflection turns into a reception. God reveals to the quiet heart and silent mind the mystery of his will and loving design. Here we come to remember the very purpose of life.

What reminders come to us in prayer? That God is deeply in love with us, his people, and longs to share his life with us; that we are created in his image and likeness; that sin causes great distancing between ourselves and God, as well as between ourselves and our brothers and sisters; that Jesus came to reconcile all creation to the Father and that we participate in that very work; that the Spirit has been given to us with power and enthusiasm; that human dignity must be protected and promoted at every level. The immediacy of everyday experience tends to obscure these faith facts. Quiet reflection and gentle presence can once again put these truths back in perspective and thus make possible the evangelization process.

How can this be done in a culture that is so active and ill-disposed to stillness? Perhaps the radio and television may have to be turned off to create an atmosphere of prayer; perhaps in driving to and from the store or school we can use that space of time for pondering God's presence; perhaps an annual retreat is in order and long overdue; perhaps fifteen minutes of Bible reading every night before retiring would deepen our sense of the divine will; perhaps getting to church fifteen minutes before the liturgy would dispose us more adequately to participate in the mysteries of our faith. Creative responses are necessary if we are to protect the realm of silence in our lives.

Last November the Wisconsin sky was overcast for the better part of three weeks. Then one evening the clouds broke and the stars came out of hiding. During the gloomy weather I had forgotten these old friends. Now they caught my attention and I was held spellbound by them for several minutes. That moment of star-gazing helped me to regain a sense of perspective that had been lost because of a hurried schedule (and the clouds that overstayed their welcome). In the evangelization process we are challenged to gaze at our faith stars. These are guiding lights that provide meaning, stir us to action, and assist us on the journey. Clouds of distraction, the mist of doubt, the darkness of fear can easily hinder our faith. Prayerful reflection will help to dissipate these obstacles and provide a means of hearing the Lord's call and responding with courage and generosity.

NO EYE HAS SEEN

No eye has seen
The bodies, the brave and lustrous bodies
Walking superb
Among golden branches, seen the horses,
Winged and scarlet mounts,
Waiting to take the eternal riders,
Swift as starfire, there beside the sea
Whose breakers rise to touch the constellations.

Nor ear heard
The contrapuntal lights aloft
The glistening orchards or heard fingers play
On strings all strung across
White gardens where the lovers stroll,
Nor heard the voices of men statuesque
Scaling circular stairs,
Music as deep as love,
Taller than expectation.

Nor has it entered the heart of man
How men and women, contemplative
Of one another, touch and know
How love can rise, a mounting wave
Within them, and their eyes
Can never surfeit on each other's beauty,
While the great world, love itself,
Lifts and transports them in compulsive motion.

Brother Edward Seifert, F.S.C

The Party's Over—Or Is It?

Follow-through is an important principle in sports. In hitting the ball the golfer must follow-through (complete the swing) as fully as possible to get distance. The basketball player must follow-through (extend the arm toward the basket) to make a successful shot. Follow-through is basically the completion of an act so that it is not short-circuited. What is true of sports in this regard is also true of many other areas of life: following-through on relationships, on promises made, on the development of personal gifts. It is also applicable to our RE-NEW program.

For two and a half years we have been in the serious process of growth in our faith. During the five seasons of RENEW we have reflected on God's call, examined our response, reflected on the empowerment of the Holy Spirit, carefully looked at the mystery of discipleship and felt the challenge to continue the work of evangelization. Possibly our work is now done and we can resume our lives as they were lived before this program began. We cannot. Follow-through on the RENEW program calls us to continue the process of growth in our faith.

Our area of follow-through certainly involves *scripture*. We know the importance of the word of God. Through our Sunday liturgies, through small group discussions, through private reading of the Hebrew scriptures and the New Testament, we have come to appreciate the power contained in the Bible. At times the message was consoling: God loves us with extravagance. At times the message was confronting: the fact of sin and its destructive power. What is important is that we continue to read and reflect upon the scriptures and, if possible, to share those reflections with others. Some may continue with their small groups already formed; others will buy some of the excellent commentaries on scripture that are available at reasonable prices; others may organize new study groups and move systematically through the Bible.

A second area of following-through might be to set some *personal goals*. Each of us is called by God to grow. Personal goals of change might be in the physical dimension of our lives (more rest, better diet, some exercise); as we know, our physical health is the foundation for other human activity. Interpersonal relationships are essential to life and here, too, goals are sometimes in order: budgeting times for friendship, keeping in contact through phone or letter with distant friends, seeking counseling to resolve some tension areas. On the social or political levels there are objectives that help us to be more responsible: becoming informed on urgent national and international issues, voting responsibly, attending meetings aimed at promoting the common good. In the specifically spiritual domain we might set some goals as to the time and place for prayer, making a retreat, doing some spiritual reading daily. Goal setting is important in following-through on God's call to live life to the full.

Putting our faith into *action*! Taking the word heard, allowing it to be internalized and assimilated, then expressing it in word and deed. That last phrase is the follow-through. So we reach out to the poor, to those in prison, to the marginal and alienated. And surprisingly our own lives become enriched because we are nourished by what they have to offer to us as much as by what we have to share with them.

Two things are of special help in evangelization and the process of follow-through: specificity and accountability. Specificity means to be as concrete and as detailed as possible about what we are to do. We need to nail things down in terms of time lines and objectives. Secondly, follow-through is aided if we have someone to hold us accountable. Not to have these two ingredients can lead to a nebulous existence, one filled with all kinds of *shoulds, maybes* and *sometimes*.

The golfer knows that simply hitting the ball is not enough: there must be the completion of the swing in the follow-through. The RENEW party isn't over: we have just begun. Its success will depend upon decisions made now in continuing to hear and respond to the voice of Christ and the impulse of the Holy Spirit.

AT THE NEW YEAR

At the new year praise the unspoken,
The scarcely conceived,
Rainbows now in the making,
Poems softly simmering
Somewhere over the eyebrows,
Murals in potency, carvings
At work in the carver.

The day is full of the unbegotten,
Designs not yet cut,
Love before pulse beat,
Palest yellow that could be sunrise.

This moment now before fleshing
Lines around being,
Let us praise all the potencies
Under the sun.

                                   Brother Edward Seifert, F.S.C.

DISCUSSION QUESTIONS

God's Call

One Valentine Day
  1) Is our deepest need to be loved? Comment.
  2) What is the difference between self-giving and gift-giving?

Humpty Dumpty's Dilemma
  1) What factor does faith play in your life as you deal with difficulties?
  2) Why is love sometimes called mercy?

The Domestic Church
  1) What symbols are important to you in your home/family?
  2) What distinguishes a faith community (family) from a human community (family)?

Lest The Parish Perish
  1) What is to happen in a parish—what happens in yours?
  2) What is the relationship between the parish and the family?

He Ain't Heavy, . . .
  1) How do you deal with mistrust, isolation and anger?
  2) List the people who reach out to you—those to whom you reach out?

Characterless Caterpillar
  1) Who are models of hope and courage in our world today?
  2) How is hope recovered and courage revitalized?

Our Response

Look Before You Leap

1) What risks have you taken in the last year?
2) Why is change so painful? Why is growth so necessary?

Moral Cancer

1) What ever became of sin?
2) What does the NCT acronym say to you?

Raised Eyebrows

1) What do you understand by unconditional love?
2) When are conditions helpful and necessary in loving?

Fill In The Blank

1) Why are commitments so difficult to make? Especially today?
2) What standards do you use in making decisions?

Where Do You Live?

1) Where and when do you find God? When is he absent?
2) What spiritual exercises are helpful to you in your attempt to remain in God's presence?

Learn a Lesson from the Redwood

1) What has been your experience of perseverance, enthusiasm and hope?
2) Will there always be unredeemed areas of our minds and hearts?

Empowerment Of The Holy Spirit

You Do What?

1) What does God do? In scripture, in your life?
2) Is your job description as a Christian essentially the same as the Spirit's?

The Power And The Glory

1) Do you assume your proper power and responsibility as a Christian?
2) Is weakness an imperfection?

Mission Impossible

1) What do you see as the mission of the Church?
2) Who is responsible for achieving that mission?

Spitballers Beware

1) What is the connection between love and justice?
2) What gospel stories bring out Jesus' concern for justice?

One Of These Days

1) What blocks you from accomplishing the mission of the Church?
2) What roles does the Spirit play in removing roadblocks on our journey?

No Utopian Camelot

1) Why are false expectations so destructive?
2) What tensions and struggles do you contend with on the journey?

Discipleship

R.S.V.P.

> 1) Who is called to discipleship? Why?
> 2) Are disciples also friends of the master Jesus?

The Lone Ranger Is Dead

> 1) Why is individualism contrary to discipleship?
> 2) How does community help the disciple?

A Vitamin A Day Keeps . . .

> 1) What nourishes you as a disciple of Jesus?
> 2) How can we ruin our health as disciples? What are the dangers?

How Much Does It Cost?

> 1) What is the role of suffering in discipleship?
> 2) Is joy compatible with suffering?

Scars Revisited

> 1) List some healing moments in your own life.
> 2) What happens if memories are not healed, sins not confessed?

Taking The Stand

> 1) When have you witnessed your faith in a public setting?
> 2) How is our mission like/unlike the mission of Jesus?

Evangelization

The Infection Of Faith

1) Explain: "change of lords."
2) Why is the living of faith so difficult?

Will It Fly?

1) Do you have to deal with cultural despair?
2) What is the relationship between God's initiative and our cooperation in the evangelization process?

Once Upon A Time . . .

1) Share part of your own faith story.
2) How does Jesus' story become our own?

There's Room In The Inn

1) Do you experience discrimination in your life?
2) What are the characteristics of the hospitable person?

Star-Gazing

1) How does one sustain a sense of wonder and awe?
2) What happens when we fail to consistently reflect upon life and faith?

The Party's Over—Or Is It?

1) How can you continue the RENEW process in your own life?
2) How are the sacraments a process and not just a point in time?

SPIRITUALITY AND HUMAN GROWTH

An eight-cassette program recorded at a three-week workshop at St. Norbert College brings a remarkable blending of deep spirituality, fine literary awareness and sensitivity and a theological-historical awareness of 14 subjects. The awareness of humanness, the humor and the remarkable organization of these talks translate well into a significant program.

TAH097 —   14 talks on 8 cassettes with outlines - **$59.95**
        Each cassette is available separately at **$7.95**

Loneliness/Growth; Person/Meaning; Courage/Longing; Suffering/Death; Creativity; Intimacy; Weakness/Time; Joy/Contemplation.

SPIRITUALITY AND SOCIAL JUSTICE

Spirituality and social justice are two sides of the same coin: love of God and love of neighbor. Indeed "any spirituality which neglects the demands of fraternal love and concern—even the demands of love for one's enemies—cannot be authentically Christian" (Thomas Green, SJ). This series of lectures illustrates with wit and insight how spirituality and social justice are inextricably intertwined.

1. *Twin Circles—To act justly*
2. *To love tenderly—To walk humbly with God*
3. *The Portrait of a Just Person—Mater et Magistra*
4. *Pacem in Terris: Justice & Peace & the Spiritual Life*
   Laborem Exercens: Work as an Issue of Spirituality & Justice
5. *Familiaris Consortio: Family Life, Spirituality & Justice*
   The Faith that does Justice
6. *The Importance of Christology*
   The Church—the Kingdom—Society
7. *Justice: A Catscan—Principles of Discernment*

TAH130—Complete set of 7 C90 tapes in dustproof shelf-case with
             outlines—**$53.95**

Available at your local BOOK STORE or from:
     Alba House Publications
     2187 Victory Blvd.
     Staten Island, N.Y. 10314-6603